*"Dear God,
It Hurts!"*

❧

"Dear God, It Hurts!"

Comfort for Those Who Grieve

William and Patricia Coleman

VINE
BOOKS

SERVANT PUBLICATIONS
ANN ARBOR, MICHIGAN

Vine Books is an imprint of Servant Publications especially
designed to serve evangelical Christians.

Unless otherwise indicated, all Scriptures quotations are from the
Holy Bible, New International Version, © 1973, 1978, 1984 by
International Bible Society. Used by permission of Zondervan
Publishing House. All rights reserved. Verses marked KJV are
from the *King James Version* of the Bible; verses marked TLB are
from *The Living Bible.*

Published by Servant Publications
P.O. Box 8617
Ann Arbor, Michigan 48107

Cover photograph: © Gabe Palmer/The Stock Market.

02   03   10   9   8   7   6   5   4

Printed in the United States of America
ISBN 1-56955-192-8

Cataloging-in-Publication Data on file at the Library of Congress.

With Appreciation

We want to thank the many people who encouraged us in the writing of this book. Their enthusiasm and heartfelt sense of need for the project have spurred us on.

Especially we want to thank Heidi Saxton, senior editor at Servant Publications. Her helpfulness and insight have made this work possible.

As a counselor I (Bill) hear many stories of loss. We have been careful not to use any of the material from my clients in this book.

Table of Contents

Introduction

Forest fires leave terrible destruction and loss. They burn and kill much of what lies in their path. Ashes, smoldering embers, and charred logs remain as stark reminders of their passing.

Fortunately, buried beneath the ruins are tiny green seedlings. These seedlings speak of hope and life for tomorrow as they begin to grow into strong and beautiful trees.

This book was written to help us look for the seedlings. Our losses are real. Our pain is deep. We can't chase those away. Yet with the grace of God we can begin to find signs of life. We may even be inspired to plant a few new seedlings of our own.

Bill and Pat Coleman
Thanksgiving Week, 1999

MaMa Tingle

Children suffer not (I think)
less than their elders,
but differently.

C.S. Lewis

As a child, visiting Grandmother Tingle's house was heaven on earth to me. Her home in eastern Maryland was only eleven miles from ours. My brother, sister, and I often spent weekends there. Sometimes we all went together, and sometimes, on special occasions, we went one at a time.

Her entrance steps had been specially crafted by my uncle. They were wide and deep enough for us to spend hours on them, playing house or store. Next to the steps, beautiful bushes gave host to delicate white flowers during the hot summers.

In the spring MaMa Tingle and I would walk through the nearby woods to pick buckets of wild blackberries. Back at her house I'd watch as MaMa effortlessly rolled out dough to make juicy cobblers. She would let me work in the kitchen with her, shaping biscuits and marking them with the prongs of a fork before popping them into the oven.

The neighborhood was sprinkled with aunts, uncles, and cousins. We visited them often.

When I was thirteen, MaMa, who had never been sick, seemed unable to get over a cold. Dad and we children were put in charge at our house while Mother went to stay with her for a few days.

Then the phone call came. MaMa was dead. Stunned, I felt as if my world stood still. The secure life I had known was over. How could Grandmother be gone? She had always been there. I couldn't begin to understand it. My life was shattered, and I felt like part of me was gone forever.

Back in those days bodies were laid in state at home. Family, neighbors, and friends came to the house. I remember standing by the coffin, feeling empty and lost.

Cousin Mary came up beside me. She wrapped her arms around my shoulders. Gently, she pulled me to her and let me cry and cry and cry.

Today, many years later, I still go back to the cemetery beside the little country church. I pause beside MaMa's grave and I remember. I remember how much we loved each other, and I think about how much she added to my life during the first thirteen years.

A Rose on the Table

Shelly would have relished this in the same way she had enjoyed most events: with a wide smile, eager eyes, hair brushed back in her own peculiar way. The peppy teen would have stood erect and marched confidently on graduation day.

Unfortunately, this was a celebration she could not attend. Instead, a single rose in a slender vase occupied its place on a table on a platform in an auditorium.

Seniors lined up to collect diplomas, awards, and scholarships. But Shelly's gown would go unworn. Her seat in the chorus would be vacant.

A rose at graduation is a solitary statement. It says that someone didn't make it. A car hit a tree, a cure couldn't be found, surgery could not mend what was torn forever. Maybe a bullet exploded through flesh and bone, leaving a young body on the night pavement.

Following the ceremony the hall would empty

and the crowd in the parking lot would quickly thin out. Parties, barbecues, presents, and excited relatives would mingle as laughter rang through homes dotted across town. A handful of her relatives would pick up Shelly's flower, force smiles, shake a few hands.

Death stole her away from her family and robbed classmates of her company. Life takes an uneasy step forward.

The rose on the table bids a quiet farewell.

But as for me, I know that my Redeemer lives,
and that he will stand upon the earth at last.
And I know that after this body has decayed,
this body shall see God!

JOB 19:25-26, TLB

When You Both Grieve

There is no limit to human suffering.
When one thinks,
"Now I have touched the bottom of the sea—
now I can go no deeper,"
one goes deeper.

Katherine Mansfield

*O*ften grief is unequal for couples. When an elderly mother dies, both husband and wife may be sad, but they do not grieve in the same way. After all, she was actually the mother to only one, the husband or the wife.

Usually the one who is suffering less is able to come to the relief of the other. That's the way it normally works with married couples.

But Angela says it's different when a teen dies.

The sudden death of their son, Brandon, left her and her husband equally devastated. They weren't able to hold one another well because each was in too much pain to support the other.

"When we were told that Brandon had died, it was like we each were hit with a sledgehammer. Shattered to the core, we were simply not able to provide comfort for each other."

In their suffering Angela and her husband were unable to reach out to each other for guidance. They did not connect with a minister, a counselor, or even a wise elderly aunt. They hurt. They moved apart. They blamed. They accused. They eventually divorced.

Two good people who loved each other and loved their son were overwhelmed by grief and couldn't sort it out. Unfortunately, this is often true of parents who lose a child. Without proper help they frequently find it too hard to continue together.

Anyone who buries a child is destined to carry crippling pain. There may be few deaths worse than this. Some rise up and carry the pain with determination. Others fall beneath its weight. Some spend their energies dealing with the grief, sorting it out, understanding it, and turning it into something meaningful. Others aim their energies at each other and destroy their relationship without ever meaning to.

Fortunately, for most of us the occasions to grieve are rare. Grieving isn't part of our normal routine. Since we see it so infrequently, we aren't particularly good at it. Thus we may hold back, blame others, or express ourselves in destructive ways.

Those who handle grief best may be the ones who turn to a minister, a counselor, or a friend.

No bond in closer union knits two human hearts than fellowship in grief.

Robert Southay

The Elephant's Heart

*T*he newspaper carried a story about an elephant who grieved until she couldn't go on anymore. Damini was seventy-two years old when a young, pregnant elephant named Champakali was brought to her zoo in India.

Damini was drawn to her new acquaintance. Not an uncommon practice among pachyderms, the older female watched carefully over the vulnerable youth. The pair bonded, as their counterparts often do in the wild. Authorities agree that elephants develop emotional ties to each other. Elephants like elephants and often create healthy social groups.

When the time came for Champakali to deliver her calf, complications were apparent. On a spring day, while giving birth, the hopeful mother died. Her calf was stillborn. A sense of loss hung heavy over the area.

Zookeepers believe they saw tears in old Damini's eyes. According to the report, Damini moped around and hardly touched her large meals. Bananas didn't entice her as they once had. Grass was seldom touched. Soon she stopped caring about food altogether

Eventually Damini lay down and seemed to give up. Her eyes were sad and wet. Veterinarians rushed to the rescue, but to little avail. Injecting vitamins into her system had no lasting effect.

Within a month of Champakali's death Damini's body also ceased to function. She was gone.

True, she was old. True, she may have had health problems. But just as true, the aging elephant also had her heart broken by the death of a being she cared very much about.

Animal lovers won't have much trouble believing this story. They have watched a cat's behavior when another cat has died. They have listened to a dog mourn or seen a horse search around with sadness. Animals lovers are believers.

People and animals are not the same. Don't bother to argue the technicalities. Yet there is plenty to suggest that nature sometimes expresses a profound sense of loss when something has been torn away and cannot be replaced.

Grieving is a natural process and raises its sad head in some of the most unlikely places. Even elephants accept matters of the heart.

Every heart has its own ache.

Thomas Fuller

Her Lost Son

It is only in sorrow bad weather masters us;
in joy we face the storm and defy it.

Amelia Barr

My first memories of Grandma Daisy are of an elderly woman in a bonnet. A conservative lady who attended the local Brethren Church, she left no scandalous things to talk about. The biggest piece of gossip I know personally is that I saw her drink a beer at the beach one hot summer afternoon.

Her husband, my grandfather, worked hard at the stone quarry. It was a dangerous job, and the dust must have taken a toll on his health, though he lived to a ripe old age.

As for Grandma Daisy, she was busy birthing and raising thirteen children. Two of them died in their youth. The other eleven went on to live productive lives. Number thirteen, the kid in the family, was my dad, Marion.

Grandma kept house, raised a garden, and stayed busy with all the good things a rural mother did in those days in Carroll County, Maryland. My guess is that her thirteen children were her social life, her hobbies, and her exercise classes. She packed them all off to church on Sundays.

I suppose my dad's life was fairly uneventful. He graduated from the eighth grade and helped teach for a while. Then, as a teenager, Marion lied about his age, joined the Navy, and took off.

So far the story isn't too amazing. Many young people have done this.

With a houseful of children to feed, clothe, and train, how disappointed could Grandma have been when her youngest left? Yet I was astonished to learn that Grandma Daisy wasn't pleased at all. When she heard what upstart Marion had done, she immediately began a search for him. She made contacts. She pushed the issue. And soon her son (did I mention that he was number thirteen?) was turned around in California and sent back home to his mother.

Why, I have often wondered, would a mother of thirteen reach out and pull back a son merely because he enlisted in the service too early? Shouldn't she have been relieved to push the last one out of the nest?

Now I realize what must have been true. A loss is a loss. A lost child is a lost child. There are no extra ones. Everybody is important.

Thanks, Grandma Daisy. Now I get it.

Suppose one of you has a hundred sheep and loses one of them. Does he not leave the ninety-nine in the open country and go after the lost sheep until he finds it? And when he finds it, he joyfully puts it on his shoulders and goes home.

LUKE 15:4-6

Grief fills the room up of my absent child,
Lies in his bed, walks up and down with me,
Puts on his pretty looks, repeats his words,
Remembers me of all his gracious parts,
Stuffs out his vacant garments with his form.

Shakespeare

Between the grief and nothing I will take grief.

William Faulkner

Since every death diminishes us a little,
we grieve —
not so much for the death as for ourselves.

Lynn Caine

Remembering Our Friends

Laugh and the world laughs with you;
Weep, and you weep alone;
For the sad old earth must borrow its mirth,
But has trouble enough of its own.

Ella Wheeler Wilcox

*E*mily and Michelle expected to be friends forever. Once a month they went shopping, got a bite to eat, and caught a movie. Often their families got together. They were comfortable in each other's company.

Unfortunately, life began to unravel for Michelle. She lost the job she had held for years and had to begin all over again in an entry-level position. The change seemed to affect her personality.

In the middle of this stress her husband, Gary, had an affair. His unfaithfulness crushed this already bruised reed.

Angry and bitter, Michelle had little good to say about life or any of its facets. Every conversation was nasty and ugly. If Emily failed to see the world through the same dark, angry glasses, Michelle became impatient and ill-tempered toward her friend. Emily continued to call, but Michelle was never available to go out. Accidental meetings were cut short as the wounded friend bristled away.

The once happy friendship could not survive such pressure. Bewildered and hurt, Emily grew to accept the obvious and reluctantly looked for other pursuits.

As difficult as it may be to admit, many of us have had experiences similar to this. We spend years getting close to someone and then something foreign comes between us. It is like a virus or a tiny worm working its way into a relationship. Undetected, it slowly destroys the tissue that holds the friendship together.

Many of us are left to grieve the loss of a living person. Yesterday they were here, today they are gone; and yet they are still alive and functioning. What kind of crazy world is this?

It happens. And when it does, we are far better off to concentrate on the good years, when we laughed and cried together. If we dwell instead on the loss, we will only cloud over and blur the rich fellowship we once knew. Eventually we will even deny that we were ever close.

Smart people lock the healthy memories in their hearts and throw the key away. Some friends will come and go, but how much they meant to us remains forever.

Sorrow [that is] fully accepted brings its own gifts.

For there is an alchemy in sorrow.

It can be transmuted into wisdom.

Pearl S. Buck

Love Hurts

*I*f you love baseball, you are going to be disappointed. Your team will go into a slump; your hero will strike out with the bases loaded. The ancient cry of "Wait till next year" will sometimes grow old and wear thin.

Anyone who has loved a pet knows the same disappointment. Sweet little Marris the Cat can have a bad temper and develop a nasty attitude. She might even forget where she is supposed to do her "business."

No matter the object of our love, the most certain result will eventually be the feeling of hurt. Human love will always be imperfect, and the imperfection of love will find a way of letting us down, disappointing us, and leaving us with pain.

Everything has a cost. The cost we pay for daring to love is that we will certainly lose.

No love is riskier than that for another person. People are different than paintings, antique autos, or butterflies. Each of us has discovered the fluctuations that come along with flesh, spirit, and the infrequent headache. People are different than stamp collections, and consequently people are more likely to touch our hearts.

Anyone who loves his or her work more than he or she loves other people may be in need of more lessons in intimacy.

Because we love a person, hurt awaits us on the horizon, and probably not on the distant horizon at that. The person we love will be inconsiderate from time to time. That person will get sick from this or that. The surest part of any relationship is that one day we will be separated.

The two who are made one flesh will not always be. Physically we will be torn asunder, and that very tearing will be painful beyond description. The price we pay for love is high.

Most of us know that. Maybe all of us. We may not know how much it will one day hurt, but we know it will hurt. And we choose to love anyway.

Some have had a disastrous love and, looking back, are not sure if it was worth it. But blessed is the person who has dared to love, with all his or her heart, and later has known it was worth every minute of the pain.

In fact, the pain, to those who love deeply, pales

in comparison to all the joy and satisfaction. Looking back, they say, "If I had known how much my pain would be, I would have chosen to do it all over again."

That's how much they have loved.

The truth that many people never understand, until it is too late, is that the more you try to avoid suffering the more you suffer because smaller and more insignificant things begin to torture you in proportion to your fear of being hurt.

Thomas Merton

He will yet fill your mouth with laughter
and your lips with shouts of joy.

JOB 8:21

There is no rainbow without a cloud and a storm.

J.H. Vincent

Lest I Lose Myself

❦

Watch for emotional, spiritual, or behavioral regressions when you are most vulnerable. Try to avoid, minimize, or stop your regression.

Morrie Schwartz

*B*ernie must have it made," I observe to no one but myself. Extremely extroverted, talented, and successful, he apparently has money enough to burn. Every now and again when I pause to pout, my green, envious eyes come to rest on this person I barely know.

Normally I am enthused about what I do, fairly content with who I have become. But occasionally I take the destructive route of wishing I were someone else.

The truth is, there is only one way for me to walk the path of envy and jealousy. I must make the sad mistake of losing who I am. It is one thing to lose myself for Christ's sake. It is quite another to lose myself in the ugly maze of wishing I could be someone else.

There are too many things I like about who I am. I like the way I have fought some of my battles. Win or lose, I believe I often have battled wisely and intelligently. I even like the way I have continued to fail. Exhausted, pummeled, and sometimes confused, at least failure has taught me I am alive and not afraid to fight the good fight.

Am I becoming who I want to be? Pretty much. If I have rough edges, I actually enjoy some of those ragged sides. There are some things I would alter, but by and large I have made a sort of peace with most of my idiosyncrasies. I have even learned to love a few.

To lose myself, in the nonbiblical sense, would be the ultimate catastrophe. Losing my house, my car, my autographed baseball, those are trifles compared to tossing the real me into the dump.

Too many of us grieve with the saddest, woeful cry because we have lost our way and no longer know who we actually might be. How often have we sat alone, heads in our hands, lamenting our misplaced selves? Those sessions equal the most severe losses we have ever known.

Let the person with the fancy car be on his way. Dismiss the character with the perfect physique. Enough of the youth who can recite the Mongolian alphabet. Who needs what they have? I am too busy whittling away at what makes me special.

There are a few people I will miss to the core of my empty heart. I can do little about that. But what a shame it would be if I were left to mourn the loss of myself.

The self-centered suffer
   when others disappoint them.
The Christ-centered suffer
   when they disappoint others.

Leonard Ravenhill

The Doctor Said I Had It

> *If suffering is accepted and lived through, not fought*
> *against and refused ... [it] is absorbed, and having*
> *accomplished its work, it ceases to exist as suffering,*
> *and becomes part of our growing self.*
> E. Graham Howe and L. LeMesurier

No sooner had I finished buttoning my shirt than my doctor came back and invited me to join him in his office. Barely settled in the chair, I heard him speak warmly, but firmly.

"You have diabetes."

Fortunately I didn't understand all that statement included, but I did know immediately that it meant loss. A loss of independence. A loss of choice. A loss of freedom. For someone who had refused all his life to take aspirin, this was a jolt.

Remaining calm, I half-listened as the good physician rattled off instructions, handed me a copy of a diet to keep, and wrote a prescription. Bundling up my new collection of medicine samples, I headed for the door, a half-grin pasted on my face.

At first my attitude was part denial, part defiance. I knew my doctor was bright and capable, so obviously the tests must have been wrong. You read about that happening all the time. Reluctantly, I decided to go along with the program. I'd keep the diet (since my wife would prepare it) and take the pills. Soon I would be back in the clinic, and they would see that an error had been made.

Exactly as I had expected, on my next visit my numbers were improved. "See," I thought, "the numbers are half-down." Yet they were still not what they should have been. "That's all right. I'll show them," I resolved.

A year later my stubborn nature took over, and I simply stopped taking the pills. "I'm not a pill person," I told myself. Months later I returned to examining room number three, sick, weak, and tired. Finally conceding the issue, I surrendered and accepted reality.

Once I accepted the loss, I could begin to deal with it, but not until then. Evidently that's the way it is with all humans. As long as I denied my loss, I had trouble making progress.

Today I take the medicine, go for walks, look for sugar-free desserts, and rumble along. I don't use the label "diabetic," but I do have diabetes. The difference is important to me.

By accepting my loss I am able to minimize its effects. My condition does not run my life. When I am foolish enough to abuse it, however, my condition grabs me by the throat.

More losses are waiting down the road. If the diabetes doesn't do damage, something else will. Hopefully I will be able to deal with the next loss better because I have already had some experience at losing physically.

The doctor probably will have some more messages for me in the days to come. Again I will need to recognize my loss, carry on with the best I have, and thank God for what I have left.

Into each life some rain must fall,
Some days must be dark and dreary.
Henry Wadsworth Longfellow

Then Abraham gave up the ghost...
and was gathered to his people.

GENESIS 25:8, KJV

❦

There are comforts and compensations that one
who has not suffered knows nothing of . . . like the
lamps that nobody sees till the tunnel comes.

R.W. Barbour

What is unbearable is not to suffer but to be afraid of suffering. To endure a precise pain, a definite loss, a hunger for something one knows— this it is possible to bear. One can live with this pain. But in fear there is all the suffering of the world: to dread suffering is to suffer infinite pain, since one supposes it unbearable; it is to revolt against the universe, to lose one's place and one's rights in it, to become vulnerable over the whole extent of one's being.

Louis Evely

I find that all that talk about "feeling that he is closer to us than before" isn't just talk.

It's just what it does feel like—

I can't put it into words.

One seems at moments to be

living in a new world.

Lots, lots of pain, but not a particle of depression or resentment.

C.S. Lewis

The Fading Face

The light is gone from my life.
> Theodore Roosevelt
> (on the death of his first wife)

After my husband died, I felt like one of those spiraled shells washed up on the beach.... No flesh, no life.
> Lynn Caine

*B*efore he married Joy, C.S. Lewis thought he understood about the nature of death, but when his wife died shortly after their marriage, grief took on a whole new meaning. As time went on, the face of his deceased wife became a blurred memory; he could no longer see clearly the distinguished features she had when she was alive and active.

Commenting on his loss, Lewis said that he felt that he had seen his loved one in so many lights—laughing, crying, and sparkling—that when he thought of her, all of those facets rushed together. It was the joining of those expressions that detracted from the clarity.

This is not an uncommon experience in loss, but it is often bewildering. While we say we remember our lost loved ones as if they were here, not everyone feels that way. Often we mean that the love or the pain is as strong as if it were yesterday that we faced our loss, but the sharpness of the image has begun to fade.

Even good photos are not quite enough. The faces in pictures or on tapes still lack the full dimension and the vitality of the persons with whom we have shared our lives.

If we aren't careful, we may begin to feel guilty about our fading mental vision. After all, what kind of people are we, to let the memory of someone we love fade as if it were paper beginning to discolor with age?

Possibly this fading is partially a gift. Could it be that we would have more difficulty living in the here and now if the presence of our lost loved ones was as vivid as today's sunshine or this evening's stars? Some of yesterday has to draw back in order to make room for today. We might hate that fact, yet there may be considerable healing in the truth of it.

That's how we go on, how we take up the task of living tomorrow. Some of us marry again. Dream again. Learn a new skill. In order for life to march on, distance must begin to form between the fantastic memories we have and the new memories we dare to create.

We do not dishonor our loved ones by developing new pictures and new scenes. My guess is that they would be perplexed if they knew we were afraid to move on. The present comes into focus, allowing us to celebrate the moment.

And if we could see the smiles on their faces, they would probably show us that they are well pleased to see us fill up our lives with the new.

When I am dead, my dearest,
sing no sad songs for me.

Christina Rossetti

When Grieving Takes Time

*Everyone can master a grief
but he that has it.*

Shakespeare

You aren't going to simply sit around and pout, are you?" Donna spoke crisply to her fifteen-year-old son. "The divorce is almost final, Jason. You can't spend the rest of your life with a chip on your shoulder."

Jason's mother wanted him to hurry up and get over his grief. She had expected him to take it hard; however, now she was anxious to move on.

What Donna forgot was that she had a full year to get used to the idea. For some time she had known that the relationship was over. She had actively worked on the process of getting through the pain. By now she had walked out of the fog and was looking for the sunshine.

Only recently had Jason been told about the terrible death of his family. Still in shock, he was having trouble sifting out the loss.

Too often we forget that each person may be in a different stage of grief. One person may not have realized that the problem was this critical. Another may have been ignoring what should have been the obvious facts.

We do not all travel on the same train, and all trains do not roll along at the same speed. Caring people try to allow for the grieving needs of each individual.

When we demand that others "hurry up" and grieve, we are usually knee-deep in self-centeredness. We expect someone else's grief to adjust to our needs.

Sorrow is strange. Most of us hurt so badly that we tend to think only of ourselves, and of our own power to survive. Yet it is our ability to see the needs of others that speeds up our own healing. How can we help others adjust to the loss of income, the death of a relative, or the abandonment by a parent? Eventually the energies involved in helping others grieve become health-giving agents for ourselves as well.

Those who believe that grief is grief and it should follow a predictable set of stages are blind to how different and individual personalities may be.

The best way to find out how someone is handling loss is to take time and listen. If we listen carefully we are unlikely to try and hurry that person's grieving process.

While grief is fresh,
every attempt to divert only irritates.
Samuel Johnson

She never said, "Cease to grieve,"
but she grieved with me.

Isadora Duncan

Every man has his secret sorrows which the world
knows not;
and oftentimes we call a man cold, when he is
only sad.

Henry Wadsworth Longfellow

Grief is itself a medicine.

William Cowper

Too Brave!

❧

Believe in dreams. Never believe in hurts—you can't let the grief and the hurts and the breaking experiences of life control your future decisions.

Robert H. Schuller

When Tim was eleven years old the doctors told him they had no choice. Cancer was spreading in his arm, and the only hope he had was to have the arm removed. These were tough words for someone looking forward to the exciting teen years and all life might have to offer.

Tim's loving parents stood by his side. Wanting to make him strong and optimistic, they told the boy simply, "Don't let it bother you." With that stoic reassurance, he bucked up and took on the challenge. After all, he hadn't seen his family members show much emotion, so why should he? Be tough. Suck it in.

After the surgery Tim made his family proud. He was courageous and strong. During the rehabilitation and adjustment to his prosthesis he remained dedicated. Everyone hung together as the brave youth became engaged in a full and vigorous life.

Everyone seems to admire tough people who face the storm without wavering or complaining, who bite the bullet and take the pain, who play the hand they were dealt.

At nearly thirty years of age, Tim began to come apart at the seams. He found work harder each day. Too easily he canceled appointments. At other times he simply failed to show up. During the long evenings he began to sit alone and weep.

The brave little boy was now finding it terribly difficult to be the brave man. Now he was confused about what bravery really meant.

Because Tim had been forbidden the healthy exercise of crying, because he could not and would not grieve his horrible loss, he had not faced his agony and processed it. Almost twenty years later he became overwhelmed and had to open the floodgates.

That's the price we pay if we get confused about courage. True courage does not refuse to mourn its losses. We show far more bravery by facing our grief than we do by stuffing it inside and trying to ignore it.

No doubt we mean well when we tell loved ones to "grin and bear it," but too often we tell others not to show their grief because in fact we don't know how to handle their expression of emotions. What we really are saying is, "Don't let it out because I will feel uncomfortable if you do."

Loss doesn't go away. If we fail to work it out, what we usually do is store it. Imagine stacks and stacks of grief piled in the corners of our hearts and minds. Wise people move it out as it arrives rather than wait until it overloads.

A time to weep and a time to laugh,
a time to mourn and a time to dance.

ECCLESIASTES 3:4

Toughing It Out

❧

What soap is for the body,
tears are for the soul.

Leo Rosten

*F*actory work was never easy for Jan. She had grown up believing she would go to college, but somehow that never came about. Now pressing in on thirty-five, with two children to raise and a husband buried up on the hill, life seemed difficult and disappointing.

Most nights Jan stayed up late and sat in the kitchen drinking coffee alone. She had cried only once since the funeral, and Jan didn't plan to shed tears again any time soon. There were bills to pay, children to cook for, and homework to check. Tears, she figured, simply got in the way.

Jan's story is often repeated by those who feel a need to "tough it out." They bottle up their grief and try to pretend it has gone away. The fact is, however, that bottled-up sorrow almost never goes away.

The Son of God taught us, "Blessed are those

who mourn, for they will be comforted" (Mt 5:4). He understood the problem exactly. Those who hold it in and deny they have suffered loss fail to receive the healing comfort they really need.

By expressing grief, by talking about the pain, we make comfort a possibility.

We used to think this was just a man's problem. Today we know better. Many women also stifle their true feelings. In this hard, cold world they frequently decide to stonewall and "tough it out."

It's better to remind ourselves: (1) Even the brave need to grieve. (2) Grieving is a healthy, spiritual act. (3) Grieving is an exercise, and those who do it will feel better much sooner.

Jesus was certainly acquainted with grief. He suffered, his friends suffered, and his family was frequently in pain. As an authority on loss and compassion, he told his listeners that they needed to let go and grieve.

Don't pretend that everything is OK. It isn't. Someone we loved has died. That's devastating, and we will be better off if we admit it.

It's easy to become confused. Bravery, toughness, and courage are words that give us fuzzy thinking. There is a time to set all of these virtues aside, sit down, take out a box of tissues, and weep.

Crying might not be our style, but grieving needs to be. We get better by acknowledging that our loss was real and our pain is deep.

It is only the women whose eyes have been washed clear with tears who get the broad vision that makes them little sisters to all the world.

Dorothy Dix

Grieve and mourn for yourself,
not once or twice, but again and again. Grieving
is a great catharsis and comfort and a way of
keeping yourself composed.

Morrie Schwartz

The Teacher and the Marine

Kindergarten was a new adventure. It opened a wide world of recess, desks, a piano, and new people. Lots of people. I clung to my father that first day, but when he disappeared I was left to fend for myself.

Fortunately, the teacher was kind. I remember thinking she was pretty, like my mother. Soon she was singing songs with us and reading stories. As scared as I was, I knew I could trust this adult.

Not only did we have stories, there were also milk and cookies to eat and mats so we could nap. One part of the room had toys and a playhouse. Decorations covered the walls. Soon I was talking with the other five-year-olds.

But most of all, there was the teacher.

The darkest day of my early school career came unexpectedly a few months later. My teacher introduced the school principal, who broke the tragic news. Our teacher was going to be married in a few weeks to a Marine, and she would be moving away. It was 1943 and a war was going on, and she had to move on with her new husband.

It was shocking. I felt stunned. No one had told me that teachers move away. I had learned to trust her, to listen, to obey her. My teacher told me when the milk was coming and when to put on my coat; she even helped me button it.

Sadness settled in. How would I ever get to know a new teacher? I was torn apart.

A couple of days later as I walked down the hall, what did I see? Standing by the wall was my teacher; next to her, touching her hand, was a Marine. My jaw dropped.

"That's him," I thought. "The dirty dog. He's the one who has come to steal my teacher away. Does he have any idea what he's doing to me?"

Over the years I've never forgotten the teacher or the Marine. Their love was one of my first lessons in loss. Before that I did not know how transitory life could be.

My teacher had entered my life through the process of pain and adjustment. No sooner had I welcomed her into my trust than she was stolen away. People have often come and gone since, and I have learned to appreciate them while they are here.

We could never learn to be brave and patient,
if there were only joy in the world.

Helen Keller

That which we lose we mourn,
but must rejoice
that we ever had.

C.J. Wells

When Grief Isn't Going Well

*L*oss is a terrible experience. Someone who meant a great deal to you has gone away. After some time has passed, how can you tell if the grieving process is going well? Read over this short list and see how you fare.

The grieving process isn't going well if...

↝ You are so active you are afraid to sit and think.

↝ Within two months you find someone to marry.

↝ Your alcohol consumption is increasing.

↝ You are inactive and content to stay at home alone.

↝ You imagine your loved one was perfect.

↝ You can't laugh at things your loved one did.

↝ You have few emotions.

↝ Your anger has not begun to subside.

↝ You continue to lose weight without trying.

↝ You have lost your sense of humor.

Nothing becomes offensive so quickly as grief. When fresh, it finds someone to console it, but when it becomes chronic, it is ridiculed, and rightly.

Seneca

People who drink to drown their sorrows should be told that sorrow knows how to swim.

Ann Landers

Between Two Ledges

Our joys as winged dreams do fly;
Why then should sorrow last?
Since grief but aggravates thy loss,
Grieve not for what is past.

Anonymous

Monica's hopes were riding high. The twenty-two-year-old from Dallas had met Mr. Right, and her future was unfolding like a Tyler Texas rose. At least that's what she thought, until he dropped the news. After some serious soul-searching her friend had decided it was over.

Monica didn't hear exactly what he said, but the message was clear. No ring. No bells. No tomorrow. No quiet evenings by the fire. No little children playing at their feet. After going together for nearly a year, he cut her heart out and walked away.

At first the pain was almost too much to bear, but the worst part was that two months later the pain had hardly subsided at all. Every night she felt the hurt all over again.

A dedicated Christian, Monica wanted to know what God had planned for her life. She wanted to move on. But she found it impossible to be optimistic while the pain was so severe.

It was as though Monica was trying to cross a large, open chasm. With one hand she held on to the ledge of her past relationship, afraid to let go. With the other hand she grasped the future and the promise that God would go with her.

Why couldn't she begin to see the Lord involved in her life? Because she still refused to accept the facts: Her relationship was history now and nothing more than that.

For many of us it takes a long time to let go when something is definitely over. Frequently, people are still looking back and holding on a year or more after the truth should have settled in. It is this denial of the facts that keeps us hurting, sad, and filled with despair.

Often it takes a conscious, deliberate decision to help us pry our grip loose from the past. Only then can we grab tomorrow and God's direction with both hands. True, that is much harder than it sounds, but each of us must do it, no matter how difficult the task.

We ask, "Why doesn't God show me what he has planned for me? I really want to know." The answer comes back, "Because you aren't willing to put both hands on tomorrow, throw yourself over, and move on."

Imagine a person driving a wagon with two mules. Suddenly one mule has a heart attack and dies. Shocked and stunned, the driver yells at the surviving mule to get going. Why doesn't that stubborn animal continue on down the road?

First, the driver has to unhitch the dead mule. Only then will the living mule be free to go forward.

Ledge or mule, the story is the same. We have to let one go in order to let the other come to our aid.

The cheerful loser is a winner.

Elbert Hubbard

God gave burdens,
also shoulders.

> Yiddish Proverb

Noble deeds and hot baths
are the best cures for depression.

> Dodie Smith

A cherished grief is an iron chain.

> Stephen Vincent Benet

Pre-Grieving

❧

Grief can't be shared.
Everyone carries it alone,
his own burden, his own way.

Anne Morrow Lindbergh

*E*veryone is trying to slow me down," Jenny complained. "They act like I'm at high risk or something."

Jenny had lost her husband four months before, following a battle with cancer. She had watched his body waste away for nearly a year while his spirit had remained mostly strong.

"It's almost as if I'm too active, too happy. They think people who recover too quickly are bound to crash."

Two weeks after the funeral Jenny was back at work at the bank and becoming involved in community affairs as before.

"What most of them fail to see," she continued,

"is that I had a long time to grieve. Too long. Tim began to die on a certain day in July. His death only became completed on that Saturday afternoon in May."

Our society through history has had strong feelings about the grieving process. Widowers and widows were expected to mourn for a designated amount of time and even to wear certain clothing. How long the mourning went on was supposed to be a sign of how much the survivor loved the departed spouse.

Today we know better. Grief is highly individual. One person will process it slowly. The next will come to terms more quickly. Yet each of them may have loved the deceased with equal intensity. A third person may be wise to seek out a counselor and talk through significant feelings.

Time is a major factor in the grieving process, but how much time is needed is as personal as picking out a pair of shoes. What fits one person will only pinch the feet of someone else.

Grief and time are a combination that too easily gives birth to guilt. What if I grieve too long? What if, feeling terrible, I don't think I'm grieving like I used to?

Mixing, matching, and comparing only add to our problems.

Each of us needs to mourn loss at our own pace. We should not try to copy anyone else's pattern of recovery. The length of the grieving process may depend on how early our grief began.

When someone dies a long-expected death, the waiting goes on for a while—the waiting for what has already taken place but cannot yet be properly comprehended or decently acted upon.

Shirley Hazzard

Nell

❧

Praise is the mode of love which always has some ele-
ment of joy in it. Praise in due order; of him as the
giver, of her as the gift. Don't we in praise somehow
enjoy what we praise, however far we are from it? I
must do more of this.

C.S. Lewis

Kneeling beside her, I held her hand as she slept in the geriatric chair. There was no material thing she needed. There was no gift I could give her. I felt sure I would not see her again.

"Auntie Nell, you are a wonderful person. You have been a model to me all my life.

"When I was little, you and I would cook and clean house together and weed the flower beds. I learned to carefully set the table and dust furniture. You always made work fun. You and I sewed doll clothes and made a canopy doll bed from a cigar box.

"Remember when you bought the Studebaker and all the neighbors joked that they couldn't tell if you were coming or going?

"Remember when you introduced me to Lois Lenski books?

"When my teeth needed braces, you helped locate an orthodontist. Orthodontics was a new science in those days.

"You taught elementary school for forty-five years, and I'm sure no child left your room without learning to obey. You helped shape hundreds of lives.

"My siblings and I visited you often, and we explored the big city together. You took us on trips each summer, up and down the East Coast. I owe my love of traveling to you.

"Remember the summer you took us to Vacation Bible School and the closing program was my first experience reciting in front of adults?

"Remember the time I snuck out and went to play with the neighbor, then lied to you when I came back? Thanks for punishing me.

"You always treasured family and treated relatives with great respect. You took us for visits at the homes of cousins and uncles I would not have known otherwise.

"When I was in college you invited my roommate and me to your home for weekends. You and I went to Alaska together.

"You knit baby blankets when my children were born. You attended their graduations and weddings and knit again at their children's births. Each of us has stayed in your home many times.

"Often this tune pops into my head: 'Make new friends and keep the old; one is silver and the other gold.' I often heard you sing that and other happy songs.

"My life is richer for having you as an aunt and a friend. I must return to Nebraska tomorrow, but I shall cherish this time together. I love you and I thank you."

Whether she heard in her sleep I do not know. But I know it was comforting to me to be close to her and to thank her.

Grief drives men into habits of serious reflection, sharpens the understanding and softens the heart.

John Adams

Cursing the Doctor

❧

Of all the many evils common to all men,
the greatest is grief.

Menander

Have you ever done this? Have you ever asked, "Why in the world does the doctor keep adding pills? Now he wants me to come in for a blood test. This whole two-mile walk thing was his idea." Why is it that when we are sick we treat the doctor like an enemy?

Grousing about the people who care about us and are trying to meet our needs probably goes back as far as the Garden. We hate the fact that we aren't perfect. The very hint that we need someone else's help to see us through needles at our pride and pokes at our arrogance.

When we suffer loss, the Great Doctor is our heavenly Father. He is able to strengthen and encourage, succor and care. So how do we react to his medicine? Often in the same way that we slander the dedicated, hard-working physician.

"Why didn't God do something?" we complain. "I don't need him now; I needed him then. My heart aches to the point of breaking; why doesn't he fix me? It isn't fair that I should suffer while others around simply rollerblade through life."

Often God is expected to minister in the middle of a hostile environment. It's as if we're telling him to hurry over to help us, yet shooting at him as he's coming to our aid. It's like calling a carpenter to work on your house, then addressing him as "You bumbling, knuckle-busting, ten-thumbed fool."

Most of us, it would seem, come to God because we either trust him or want to trust him. Hurt and confused, we too often flail our arms in the air in anger at the same time we are asking God to hold us.

That's all right. It's not the best, but it's OK. God can love the child who comes kicking and screaming. He slips his loving arms between our bouncing fists and reaches us anyway.

When we become angry with God, God doesn't become angry with us. He understands loss and suffering. God's heart has been broken, too, and he can identify.

The next time we are tempted to curse the doctor, we might pause and reflect on how illogical that actually is. And the next time we get terribly upset with God, we might do the same. Helping isn't easy, and God won't be surprised if a hurting person takes a few swings at him.

Suffering is nature's way of indicating a mistaken attitude or way of behavior, and to the non-egocentric person every moment of suffering is the opportunity for growth. People should rejoice in suffering, strange as it sounds, for this is a sign of the availability of energy to transform their characters.

Rollo May

When the water in the skin was gone, she put the boy under one of the bushes. Then she went off and sat down nearby,... she thought, "I cannot watch the boy die." And as she sat,... she began to sob.

God heard the boy crying, and the angel of God called to Hagar from heaven and said to her "...Do not be afraid; God has heard the boy crying as he lies there. Lift the boy up and take him by the hand, for I will make him into a great nation."

Then God opened her eyes and she saw a well of water. So she went and filled the skin with water and gave the boy a drink.

GENESIS 21:15-19

74

The Broad-Shouldered God

I have always believed that God never gives a cross to bear larger than we can carry. No matter what, he wants us to be happy, not sad. Birds sing after a storm. Why shouldn't we?

Rose Kennedy

God has broad enough shoulders to handle whatever we care to throw his way. He is like a mighty oak, and a stiff wind isn't about to affect him.

If you think you've been given a raw deal, it's better if you let God know. Tell him what you think.

When your loss seems like too much and the pain too great, it's OK to tell your Father how you feel.

Too often we feel hostile toward God over what happens, but are afraid to say so. If we feel it, however, it's all right to say it. Letting our true anger be known to God isn't really such a big deal. After all, he knows how we think anyway.

Never would God refuse to hear us out. Could you imagine the Lord telling us to "Hush"? Or saying, "Don't complain or I'll give you something to complain about"? How about, "Watch out, you might say something you're going to regret"?

There is nothing wrong with getting the anger out. Venting may be overrated, but expressing our feelings is still the healthiest way to go.

If we are angry today, even nasty, about what has happened, tomorrow we may see things a shade differently. It may take a day, a month, or maybe even a year or two, but we shouldn't be surprised if our feelings temper as time goes by. The things we accuse God of today we may thank him for, further down the road.

Every day the Lord takes the blame for things he didn't do. Storms, diseases, even riots are placed at God's door, as if he causes every fallen tree or each crashed car. Silently he listens to some of the most absurd accusations and takes it all in stride. He understands that in our pain we look for someone to blame. God has the shoulders to take whatever we give.

God doesn't punish us because we hurt and don't know how to express it. Bolts of lightning will not come crackling through the skies. Locusts will not suddenly descend upon our garden.

The people we love can take a hit. When we say something ugly or thoughtless, most of the time they respond in a caring way. They shake it off and stay close anyway. Our Lord does nothing less. He takes a hit. Sometimes he takes a lot of hits. And still he sticks around. He stays because he is God, because he understands and because he loves us. That's what we call broad-shouldered love.

The happiest, sweetest, tenderest homes are not those where there has been no sorrow, but those which have been overshadowed with grief, and where Christ's comfort was accepted.

J.R. Miller

Accidental Gifts

❧

An apple orchard smells like wine;
A succory flower is blue.
Until grief touched these eyes of mine
Such things I never knew.

Lizette Woodworth Reese

*A*nts love to crawl across the scaly skin of the pangolin. Normally an ant eater, the pangolin doesn't seem to object to having ants eat their dinner off its long, pine-like body.

As the ants eat, they clean off the skin of their natural enemy. Ants also accidently leave an important deposit of formic acid, important to the pangolin's health.

No self-respecting ant would do this on purpose. After all, the pangolin will eat him if it can. But as the ant helps itself, it also accidently helps the pointy-nosed monster.

Someone has said that grief also leaves gifts. At first they may be hard to see. Our focus, understandably, is on our loss. Our energies, our mental capacities, even our spiritual resources, are drawn to the terrible gap that is left. As time moves on, however, our vision grows wider and we begin to notice a few of the gifts our grief has left behind.

These presents are different for each of us. There are no set formulas or gifts that we should look for. Unfortunately, some gifts go unnoticed. Overlooked, they will remain sprinkled around our hearts and souls without ever being unwrapped.

Think about some of the gifts that might be available. Imagine which presents might appear out of grief.

Some receive the gift of time. Previously they took each day for granted. Now they know their days are numbered and if they want to do something, maybe they had better get to it.

Others obtain the gift of freedom. For the first time they feel at liberty to go back to school or take a job doing what they have always wanted to do.

Many receive the gift of the Spirit. Loss has brought them closer to their faith and created an interaction with their Lord and Savior.

Losing a person we love frequently reminds us of how important love is and how much love we have to give. Despite the death, we often feel strengthened to reach out and love again.

How many of us have hurriedly gone through the mail and noticed all the negative envelopes? A bill or two here, an advertisement there, an invitation to take a chance underneath. In disgust we throw the pile on the desk and start to walk away. It's then that we see the small envelope slide out of the group. Immediately we know that it's from that special person.

Wise people look at every loss closely to see if they can find any gifts. One or two are always there.

To scale great heights,
we must come out of the lowermost depths.
The way to heaven is through hell.

Herman Melville

Comfort in Sorrow

❧

To grieve alone
is to suffer most.

Talmud

*T*here is only one funeral home in our town, and the director's name is Eldon. His father was a funeral director, and so is his son.

When my father died, all sorts of indescribable emotions ran loose in my body and mind. One moment I knew exactly where I was; the next I was floating in a twilight zone. In some ways I felt in control of myself, but in others I was definitely out of it.

But back to the funeral director.

On the day of the funeral I stood by the casket, waiting to hear what I was to do next. Suddenly my eyes fixed on my father's folded hands.

It was then that I noticed the oversized leaves from the floral arrangement touching my father's bare hands. I thought, "That must itch. That shouldn't happen to my father. Leaves shouldn't be there."

Inside, my pot was boiling. I didn't say anything to anyone, but my panic level was rising.

Suddenly and unexpectedly, Eldon moved to my side. "I really should move those leaves off your father's hands," the funeral director calmly said. Instantly his professional hands shifted the flowers and solved the problem.

To this day I have wondered what Eldon knew and how he knew it. Could he see the panic in my eyes? Had I grown suspiciously quiet? How did the funeral director know exactly what was bothering me?

The memory has always been a calm and comfortable mystery. There are some people who seem to be especially sensitive to the grief others are experiencing. Thank God for their availability and willingness to do the good thing.

Even grief has its pleasant memories, generated by caring people who are willing to reach out.

When a man has compassion for others,
God has compassion for him.

Talmud

When the Stars Shine Brightest

Stargazing is a magnificent art, but to fully appreciate the beauty of the heavens, the conditions must be right. You can't simply walk out of your apartment in the city and automatically see a thousand stars glittering in the nighttime sky, nor can you practice this skill at high noon anywhere at all.

Day or night, town or country, we know the stars are shining in place, but sometimes they are hard to see.

But what happens when daylight has gone? When the good, life-supporting sunshine no longer reigns above? It is the loss of sunshine that causes the stars to shine the brightest.

Frequently it is the loss of one thing that allows us to see something else more clearly. Only when another thing is removed can we come to appreciate the wonderful presence of what remains.

A pine tree never looked so lovely as when the tree in front of it was taken down. Flowers look more vibrant in mid-September, when you know they will too soon be gone.

Walks in the park with a friend have always been uplifting and exhilarating. Yet we may not truly understand how much they mean until that friend is gone. After the loss, the old familiar path comes alive like a pop-up book. A stream, a singing bird, a shady nook—all have always been there, yet each is newly resonant. Being alone makes us realize not only what we had but also how much we have left.

Often a person who loses a job goes home and hugs a child. People who narrowly escape an accident call an old friend on the phone. And when a doctor gives us an unfavorable report, we sit and hold hands with someone whose hand we may not have held in a very long time.

The stars shine brightest when we lose the sunshine. The loss is real, but so is the newfound appreciation for what we have. That's true even if the loss is temporary and we know it's temporary. When our spouse goes away for a week, our gratitude becomes sharper even though we know our mate will return. The same is true when children go to camp, when the check doesn't come in the mail, and when we are waiting for a fever to break.

Most losses still stink. That's why we call them losses and not gains. Fortunately, God has built in a system that allows us in loss to see even better those things that remain.

Forgive Them, for They Know Not What They Say

Don't try to console a man
while the corpse is still in the house.
Sayings of the Fathers

on't be disappointed if your friends and relatives don't know what to say. Most of us fumble through a few awkward words that often miss the mark. Don't become angry because a well-meaning soul isn't able to express himself well. We humans have difficulty reaching out to each other.

A woman in Georgia said she stopped going to church because of what the minister said at a funeral. Too bad. She may have given up a vital resource over merely a poor pastor's bumbling tongue or fuzzy thinking.

Was the minister overly tired? Would he say things differently if he had them to say over again? Or did he mean his message exactly as it came across? No matter what the cause, maybe it is time to forgive the imperfect servant.

People say painful things:

"Fortunately you can still have another baby."

"Maybe God needed more angels in the choir."

"Someday you will see this was for the best."

"All things work together somehow."

Most of us make one of two mistakes when we try to comfort. Either we try to educate or we try to encourage. Each can turn sour quickly. Better goals would be to listen and to join in with the grieving one's feelings. Instead, we struggle to say just the "right" words.

When people make the difficult effort to walk over and express their "condolences," it is better not to concentrate on their words. Words are simply side issues. Instead, let your eyes rest on the person. Be thankful the individual came. Let his presence speak its volumes. Let the passion in his face do the talking.

Forgive them, for they know not what they say. They mean well. And under pressure most of us are not at our best.

We want others to forgive the klutzy things we've

said. We need people to give us plenty of wiggle room for our mistakes. The least we can do is extend that same forgiveness back to them.

Never tell anyone they look tired;
it only makes people feel worse.

Susan Blond

The Unabomber's Brother

⚜

Loss makes artists of us all
as we weave new patterns
in the fabric of our lives.

Greta W. Crosby

*D*avid Kaczynski is a man who takes risks to help others heal. His brother, Theodore, hurt a lot of people. In seventeen years that brother killed three people and injured twenty-nine others by sending bombs through the mail. David contacted the F.B.I. because he was suspicious that his brother was the murderer. Today his brother is serving a life sentence in California without the possibility of parole.

Meanwhile David is courageously contacting families of the victims and trying to help them with their grief. He tries to bring compassion to some of the people who have been hurt the worst.

This isn't the way violent and accidental deaths

normally go. Usually family members hate each other and send condemning messages back and forth. Sometimes lawyers tell the families not to contact each other, lest they create legal complications and further hostilities.

A mother and father in Ohio believed that by hating the family of the person who took their son from them they could keep alive the memory of their son. Afraid they would feel nothing, they kept the fires burning by reminding themselves of how evil the other family must be. For them to actually meet this other family would have been impossible; it would have raised the possibility that they might find not demons but fellow human beings.

Each of us must deal with grief in our own way. Some acts of reconciliation seem too painful even to imagine. Yet now and then someone breaks the gravity of sorrow that holds them down and rises to a higher plane. A letter, a note, a phone call, or a visit becomes the angel wings that carry a message of love and concern.

David Kaczynski didn't do the deed. He never made a bomb. He never took an explosive package to the post office. Nevertheless, he held the potential healing balm in his hands and he decided to use it.

Sometimes ordinary people rise up to do extraordinary tasks. Encouraged by their labors of love, many of us find the inspiration to do what we would really like to do deep down in our hearts.

Out of suffering have emerged the strongest souls;
the most massive characters are sheared with scars.
E.H. Chapin

The only cure for grief is action.
G.H. Lewes

Through glory and dishonor,
bad report and good report;
genuine, yet regarded as impostors;
known, yet regarded as unknown;
dying, and yet we live on;
beaten, and yet not killed;
sorrowful, yet always rejoicing;
poor, yet making many rich;
having nothing, and yet possessing everything.
2 CORINTHIANS 6:8-10

The Miscarriage

❧

*W*e lost the baby," Mary said as her voice trailed off in sobs.

Mary's and Gerry's hearts were broken. Their minds could not understand.

Their greatest joy had been anticipating the birth of their first child. They had loved the tiny baby growing in the womb. The baby was part of them, physically and emotionally. One minute they were pregnant and planning, and the next it was all over.

Losing their dearest treasure and joy in life shattered their lives into little pieces. They were devastated and felt like part of them was gone forever. Their bright future suddenly turned into a deep longing ache, a stabbing acute pain. Their unborn baby had died, and they had never seen his perfect little hands, heard his voice, or touched or hugged this unique human being.

This was a death with no funeral, no memorial service, and no marker.

Though Mary had eaten, rested, and exercised for

the baby, now she felt guilt and shame. Gerry looked like walking death. They had no appetites.

It was hard when they went to church and saw children. They smiled for the outside world, but inside they were dying. People around them were unaware that they were in bereavement. The pain was overwhelming when they saw families at the grocery story. It hurt when a pregnant woman walked by, when a family with a sleeping baby sat behind them in a restaurant. It was hard to read a newspaper. It was hard to watch television and see babies, children, and families. They grieved silently, in loneliness, emotionally isolated.

Somehow Gerry made it through each day at work. At night they clung to each other and cried.

Their siblings and families loved them. Their friends cared. They felt better when someone called and said, "Can I come by?"

Somehow they managed through the following months. Slowly their pain subsided. They clung to their faith that the God who watches even the fall of a sparrow cared for them. Through their grief they held on and cared for each other with great tenderness.

Now, years later, they have a growing family of

three children. This grateful husband and wife have tender hearts for couples who experience a similar loss, and they are careful to reach out in compassion and understanding.

Friendships multiply joys
and divide grief.

H.G. Bohn

Two Kinds of Lonely

❧

Striving to tell his woes,
words would not come;
for light cares speak,
when mighty grieves are dumb.

Samuel Daniel

It's one thing to spend the evening alone, remote control in hand, flipping through monotonous channels, finding nothing to watch. There is little on but an old movie you have seen twice and a cooking show featuring clams. The rest of the stations bounce along with no interest at all.

That's one kind of lonely. You have nothing to do. There is no place you care to go. You watch the clock to see when you can head off to bed. Social lonely isn't much fun, but it's doable. Tomorrow will probably be different, and you can get together with someone then.

Unfortunately, there is a second kind of lonely. It's the kind that makes your bones ache and your heart break. Intimate loneliness is having no one to share your feelings or emotions with. Like arthritis, intimate isolation hurts to the core and has trouble letting go.

This type of loneliness has a way of making us feel empty and almost useless. There is no one to tell, no one to share our hopes, fears, or dreams.

Social loneliness is superficial and fleeting. Intimate loneliness seeps into our attitudes and even floods our dreams. A telephone call might bring relief to our social perplexity. Yet time, trust, and heart connections are necessary before we can rewire our intimate contacts.

It takes a strong will to thrive if one is to find emotional intimacy again after a loss. This is not a will to live or survive but a will to thrive. Emotional intimacy is one of the strongest signs of mental health. It means we are willing to send and receive messages about how we really feel and think. As the ingredients in a banana enrich our bodies, so does emotional intimacy offer mental nutrients.

Fortunate is the person who has one or two people to whom he can open his heart. We don't need a dozen. Just one or two to keep us grounded and safe.

When we lose such a person—whether a spouse, a friend, or a sibling—to death, the grave robs us of life's treasure. Neither gold nor silver nor rubies could compare with that which has been stolen away.

Now comes the task of replenishing what is gone. We must begin the arduous job of finding someone else with whom we can share our hearts, someone else whom we can tell about our joys, our disappointments, and our faith.

This person probably won't appear in the next week or two. Then again, he or she might. We probably won't share with this person right away. Then again, we might.

We don't ask God for mansions or for boats to sail the ocean wide, but we do hope he will send us a person who will care to see what ticks inside our hearts.

*Grief can take care of itself, but to get the full value
of a joy you must have someone to divide it with.*

Mark Twain

Grief once told brings somewhat back of peace.

W. Morris

*Then maidens will dance and be glad, young men
and old as well. I will turn their mourning into
gladness; I will give them comfort and joy instead
of sorrow.*

JEREMIAH 31:13

Say It Early

❦

"If I had any advice to give," Anna said somberly, "it would be this: If you have something to say to someone who is seriously ill, you better say it early."

Anna lost her mother in death a year ago. Reflecting, she wonders how she could have handled it a little better.

"Don't believe those scenes in the movies. You know, the ones where everyone is called around the bed to say a final good-bye to Mom. That sounds good.

"What happened in our case was that in the last couple of days Mom's pain grew worse. Naturally, we pushed the doctor to give her more medicine to fight the pain. For whatever reason, Mom became incoherent and spent the last few days out of it.

"We tried to communicate. I told her how I felt and how much I loved her, but I don't know whether she heard me. She certainly didn't respond."

Most of us don't have much experience with death. Three or four family members and close friends might die over a thirty-year period. Otherwise the majority of what we know about death comes from television, plays, movies, and books. In stories there are long good-byes and dramatic moments. Movies usually don't include death scenes where the person is incoherent for three days, two weeks, or more.

In reality there are few things we can predict about the way death will arrive. The circumstances are difficult to control and the dynamics hard to imagine.

What was Anna saying? If we have something to say, and many of us do, we had better get it said now. Death is not managed as a play might be written. We do not so easily move characters and events from day to day or from room to room. Our lives cannot be rewritten and carefully delivered in the precise order we might choose.

The softly spoken speeches we rehearse repeatedly in our minds might never have the opportunity to cross our lips.

We read these words in the Bible:

How do you know what is going to happen tomorrow? For the length of your lives is as uncertain as the morning fog—now you see it; soon it is gone.

JAMES 4:14, TLB

Tomorrow is elusive and could be full of surprises. If we know what we want to say, we had better get it said.

> *Afraid! Of whom am I afraid?*
> *Not Death—for who is He?*
> *The Porter of my Father's Lodge*
> *As much abasheth me!*

Emily Dickinson

Softening the Heart

☙

O, grief hath changed me since you saw me last.

Shakespeare

When some people experience terrible trauma, the suffering leaves them halfhearted and bitter. These people form a shell in order to make sure they don't get hurt again.

Others will meet a similar fate, yet the experience leaves them with a soft, caring nature.

Each is afflicted equally, but the results are radically different.

What makes the difference? Why does one become pliable while the other becomes brittle? Which will we become?

Suffering is neutral. It has no mind of its own. Pain can hurt, steal, and even devastate, but it has no power to control one's attitude. Factors greater than loss are within an individual's ability to control.

During times of grief we need to get in touch with several key truths.

First, we must accept loss as inevitable. No matter how well we order our lives, most of the things we cherish will eventually be taken away. This is a temporal world; nothing lasts forever. Our normal existence means we will suffer loss of all kinds. Neither our goodness nor our badness can prevent us from losing what we love.

Second, since we all hurt in some way, we must recognize that we are all related through pain. We may have a number of connections, but pain is a common denominator. If we make the mistake of thinking we will not be like others, we need a reality check. Hopefully we become more sympathetic because we know our fellow travelers suffer in many of the same ways. By acknowledging other people's pain, we are better able to deal with our own.

Third, we need to reconnect with our belief in the grace of God. It is his grace that offers us the ability to thrive in the midst of pain. Our faith in a heavenly Father can help remove bitterness. A soft heart remains open to love and can feel and care because it knows we do not deal with harsh reality by ourselves.

Because we receive and accept God's grace, we are able to extend that grace to fellow sufferers. Hard hearts have eluded the grace of God and are therefore unable to pass it on.

To have a soft heart is not an easy choice. Those of us who have made this choice understand and sympathize with those who have not gotten there quite yet. For most this does not come lightly. Yet as we become increasingly aware of others' pain, it is a little easier each day to let go of our own pain enough to let the healing grace flow in.

She knew that no human being is immune to sorrow and she wanted me to be tough, the way a green branch is tough, and to be independent, so that if anything happened to her I would be able to take hold of my own life and make a go of it.

Ilka Chase

When Friends Don't Come Through

❧

Then they sat upon the ground with him silently for seven days and nights, no one speaking a word; for they saw that his suffering was too great for words.

JOB 2:13, TLB

Sixteen-year-old sons aren't supposed to get arrested, and they certainly aren't supposed to go to jail. Yet that's exactly what happened to Tony's oldest boy. The judge sentenced him to six months in a juvenile center. Problems like that didn't run in Tony's family, and he didn't know where to turn.

This was a pain unlike any other. It wasn't a natural loss like a disease or a death. Tony had seen it coming, but try as he might there had been no way to turn it around.

This distraught father had a handful of close friends plus a few on the outer circle. Tony was sure they would come through and let him know they felt for him. He was certain. Then he was surprised.

Like giant turtles, his friends drew their heads into their shells; like wolves, they walked by in the shadows. Each one seemed awkward and uncomfortable.

At first Tony was bewildered. Then his bewilderment turned to a dull ache. Once in a while he flirted with anger. Why didn't they *say* something?

Uneasy with the silence, Tony tried to think it through. He knew most men aren't comfortable with feelings. He also realized that often they aren't good with words. They prefer sports, statistics, and automobiles. Tony admitted that he, himself, wasn't exactly skilled at helping others in their losses.

His friends didn't know what to say, so they said nothing. Few men are famous for their listening ability. If they don't have to be around suffering, they normally take the first bus out.

When Tony reminded himself what he was like and what many men are like, he was able to accept the awful truth. Most men are miserable at feelings.

With everything else he had to deal with, this brokenhearted father knew he had to let go of his disappointment. Expecting his friends to understand or to listen was simply asking too much. He felt sorry for them, and he loved them anyway.

Tough times are just that. They are tough. Too often, in the midst of despair, the people we really hope will come through don't.

The best route is always to forgive them. The truth is, they have a basic handicap. Having great trouble contacting their own feelings, they certainly aren't able to get in touch with someone else's.

Men are still good for some things, however, like baseball stats and heavy lifting.

Look What You've Learned

❧

If you were healed of a dreadful wound,
you did not want to keep the bandage.

Ursula Reilly Curtory

Once a year Troy teaches a class at his local church. Eight weeks, eight sessions. Then he waits until the following year to teach it again.

A dozen or so people gather in a small classroom to discuss the subject of loss and how it affects them. One or two people are divorced. Someone else lost his business this year. A middle-aged lady had her left arm amputated because of cancer. She wasn't sure she should come, but she is glad she did.

No heavy curriculum is presented. No three-page handouts on the theory of loss and healing. This isn't necessary. Each person in the room has lost something, and through the experience has learned. For an hour and a half each week their goal is to share lessons from the school of hard knocks. No one is the great authority. The person whose loss is only a week old has as much to offer as one whose experience was a decade ago.

The key ingredient is that each person has suffered. Out of that suffering each is willing to take a risk by teaching and learning.

Loss is bad enough by itself. The greater loss is failing to bring some good from the pain. That would leave a vacuum, and emptiness hurts too badly.

Classrooms and prearranged settings aren't for everyone. However, human contact helps the healing by leaps and bounds. One person is good at writing notes to someone he or she knows. Another person is a master at using the telephone to deliver a message. No matter the medium, the fact remains: we all heal more quickly if we find someone else to help.

Troy doesn't teach the class all year round. His life has far more to it than just loss. Nor does he buttonhole people in the corridor and say, "How'd you like to hear how my loss is coming along?" He's far too cool and collected for that.

Every person can learn from loss. If one is fortunate, one crosses paths with another person who is an excellent listener. Those experiences are too valuable to push under a basket.

Light cries out to be seen. That's why its rays sneak through the cracks and flood over the stadium. Once we have received light, we look for ways to pass it on.

More Than Once

He will wipe every tear from their eyes. There will be no more death or mourning or crying or pain, for the old order of things has passed away.

REVELATION 21:4

When Dad died, Mother and my siblings and I were devastated. He meant so much to all of us, and he was too young to leave. We missed his stability, strength, and presence. We wondered how Mother and our young sister would get along without him. How could we carry on the farm?

Obviously Dad could not have gone on living, because his lungs were so deteriorated and breathing was such agony for him. We grieved, took care of the necessary details, and worked to move on to the next stage of our lives. But our grieving was not over.

Many times in the forty years since his death, I have felt a great emptiness. When our children were born, I missed him. They would never know their wonderful grandfather, who had loved children so much. When I wondered how to raise our children, I wished I could talk to him. When we had career choices to make, Dad, with his wisdom, was not there to help. When times were hard, I wished Dad could tell me about the hard times he had gone through. When I became overwhelmed and felt inadequate for tasks, I knew Dad's calm and patient approach would have helped me find my way. I missed the extended family; they had been a big part of our growing up years, but without Dad we seldom got together. I had lost a very precious and hallowed place.

Sometimes I just needed a place to go to find my bearings again, but our home, the farm, Dad sitting at the dinner table, those things were gone.

Dad, why did you go so young? I needed you. I still need you. Life has many mysteries, and there is a lot I can't figure out. Yet, this I know: from time to time I have to work through your death again. I have to sit quietly and remember how much you meant to me, and thank you for the years we had. I'm glad I know that I have to work through grief more than once, so that I can better handle the times when it hurts.

No man is an island, entire of itself; every man is a piece of the continent, a part of the main. If a clod be washed away by the sea, Europe is less, as well as if a promontory were, as well as if a manor of thy friends or of thine own were. Any man's death diminishes me, because I am involved in mankind. And therefore never send to know for whom the bell tolls; it tolls for thee.

John Donne

Death as Birth

❧

I tell you the truth, unless a kernel of wheat falls to the ground and dies, it remains only a single seed. But if it dies, it produces many seeds. The man who loves his life will lose it, while the man who hates his life in this world will keep it for eternal life.

JOHN 12:24-25

*I*f a seed doesn't die, it can never really live. That's what Jesus Christ taught us hundreds of years ago. Not only is it a principle of nature, but it's a spiritual axiom as well.

A tree is a tree as long as it lives. During its life a giant oak or a cottonwood supports and relates to a wide variety of nature forms. When the tree dies, it becomes a "snag" and takes on an entirely new identity. A snag can nurture more than four hundred different types of life forms.

By looking closely we can see how the death of a

human being can also be a birth. Until we die there is an entire spectrum of spiritual life that we can never fully know. We have to find release from this body in order to be born into the next life.

This life can be tremendously confining. Aching joints, fading eyesight, restricted movement, and diseased bodies are each a part of this limited existence. There are plenty of benefits that we derive in this mortal vessel, but they cannot compare to the freedom awaiting us after our next birth.

If we could, many of us would hold our dying friends back and keep them on this planet. Yet in our calmer moments we know how irrational that would be. Keeping them here will only prevent their release. If they have spent their allotment of days, why stop them from a decent delivery to a place where they will reach a fuller life?

It takes faith to believe the death-to-birth concept. First, we have to believe there is a spiritual existence beyond this temporary shell. Second, we must accept the fact that our friend or relative has a place reserved in the next life. Believers in Jesus Christ are often able to pass from death into birth with confidence.

Death is too frequently described as "the end"

or "the final resting place." These phrases we accept far too easily. Our faith would better describe death as a beginning, a passing over or a transition into eternity. People of hope could be stronger if we spoke as if we had hope.

Some of us have trouble accepting a new life concept. That's all right at first. The pain and grief may be too heavy and too dark to allow any light in at first. As we become more used to the idea that death has happened, however, we may then be able to welcome the thought of a new birth.

The Fear of Losing

Father, into your hands I commit my spirit.

LUKE 23:46

By the time John, Lisa, and Ben had all crowded into their teen years, their mother was a nervous wreck. The thought of her children leaving home was causing her tremendous anxiety. She could picture them propelling out of the house like popcorn from a hot popper.

The high school years saw the mother in a continuous state of tension. "What will they do when they leave? How will I cope at home without them? What if they aren't ready? Should they go to college or not?" Hardly a day went by that she didn't work diligently at weaving webs and worrying.

Worse than the worrying were the wasted good times. Instead of opening up and enjoying what she had, the mother dedicated her energies to fretting over what she was afraid she would lose.

This mother isn't much different than the rest of us. She had some simple choices. She could either stare at the potential loss or grab hold of the present satisfaction. Like many of us, she opted for the fears of tomorrow.

We always lose what we love. There is no way to avoid it. Even if the loss is merely for a short time, it is a loss nevertheless. It is the one constant in every relationship. Yet when we concentrate on the loss, we only make it a double one. We will lose that relationship in the future. There is nothing we can do to change this. The tragic loss is to fixate on it and lose today in the bargain.

Life is enjoyed to its fullest if we are motivated by our hopes. Life is at its shallowest when we are shackled by our fears. Fear does funny things to us. Sometimes it actually becomes our protector. At other times, however, fear is nothing more than a ruthless thief, stealing from us the true value of life.

Fear is founded on the basis of inadequacy. I fear because I believe I cannot measure up to the challenge of the setback. How will I handle myself after the dreaded loss takes place?

That's where faith fits so well. In the stark reality of loss we are reassured that we are not alone. The heavenly Father we trust and believe in will not ask us to carry on by ourselves. When something or someone is taken from us, we must look to the One who will never leave us or forsake us.

Close to the End

A poor man is shunned by all his relatives—
how much more do his friends avoid him!
Though he pursues them with pleading,
they are nowhere to be found.

PROVERBS 19:7

*T*he remarkable actress Meryl Streep fell in love with a young man early in her acting career. According to several reports, John was also an actor and the two grew very close. Streep's craft was opening into full bloom and later would include such remarkable works as *The Deer Hunter, Sophie's Choice,* and *Silkwood.*

Unfortunately, as her star began to rise she learned that John was suffering from incurable bone cancer. Instead of moving away from this terrible pain, Meryl embraced the coming death.

Toward the end of John's life, Meryl took a room

in the hospital, to be close to the one she loved so dearly. Reading and laughing together became part of their regular routine. Streep used her talent to speak like different characters as she shared herself in those last days.

While many of us choose to participate in the lives of the ones we love, too often we separate ourselves during death. Uncomfortable with loss and the final moments on earth, we are tempted to build walls between our dying loved ones and ourselves.

Sometimes we should stop our world while we say good-bye. The other things we do may not be nearly as important as the opportunity to bid farewell to someone who really matters. A faithful parent, a caring grandparent, or a loving spouse is far more important than many of the mundane, monotonous events that occupy our days.

"Seeing someone off" can be a great enrichment to our souls. Such contact allows our love to work its way through to the very end. Frequently we see people off when they take a plane or board a train. We want that personal touch even though we will see them again soon. Most of us believe we will see our dying loved ones again, even though we have little idea of when this will occur.

The problem with funerals is that the honoree has already left. We attend those celebrations to show respect for the deceased and the family. But possibly we demonstrate greater love by being around to see the dying one off.

A caring person told his dying friend he would not be there for the funeral. He had had to decide between being there now or coming later for the service, he explained. He had chosen to arrive in time to say good-bye.

"If Only I Had ..."

❧

The fact is, we cannot truly face life until we have learned to face the fact that it will be taken away from us.

Billy Graham

It sounds like the chorus of a song. When it comes to my education, "If only I had ..." When I think about my children, "If only I had ..." Looking at my health today, "If only I had ..."

This is a catchy little tune; many of us sing it over and over again. This haunting refrain could be applied to much of our lives. Drenched with regret, the plaintive little phrase is sure to take us straight to the dumper, especially if we sing it frequently.

Regrets are hard to argue with. Who can find a time when we were perfect? We could have done more. We could have done better. We could have given it one more try. Regrets are like stars. There will always be plenty to count.

When someone dies, there is always more we could have said; there are more times when we could have been there; there is more time we could have devoted to prayer; there are more hours we could have spent by the bed. Any attempt to dissuade us of this would only fall on deaf ears.

Regrets can be tossed away only by their owner. No one can be talked out of them. No crowbar will wrest them away. If we embrace regrets to our chest, we can hold on to them for the rest of our lives. We will always be able to make the case that we came up short, and convince ourselves of our own inadequacies.

To remain healthy, we need to scoop up our regrets and walk down to an imaginary sea. Standing by the shore, we must begin to toss our regrets into the rippling waters, one at a time, if it helps, or by handsful or armsful if need be. All our regrets, both those put upon us and those of our own making, need to be cast into the waves.

Arms filled with regrets have no room for love. Hands that are clutching regrets can never reach out to others. They must be emptied so that they can be wrapped around those who need them.

"If only I had ..." may become the chorus that

stops us from singing, "Look what I'm going to do today." One has to be careful what kind of tune gets stuck in one's heart.

Godly sorrow brings repentance that leads to salvation and leaves no regret, but worldly sorrow brings death.
2 CORINTHIANS 7:10

The Luxury of Grief

❧

The ocean has its ebbings—
so has grief.

Thomas Campbell

A nna would have grieved longer if she could have. Three children and a responsible job prevented her from drinking too deeply from the cup of sorrow.

It was best for the children to be back in school by Monday. They would need clothes and lunch money and homework up-to-date. Friends and relatives helped, but a mother's careful eye was most important.

Her job would wait, and yet it wouldn't. The time she had taken off for her husband's illness had taken a toll at work, and already she was moving outside the circle. Besides, work was good for her, she felt, and she didn't want the boss to forget her.

Everyone is forced to taste sorrow. Sometime or other we will even have to drink deeply from its well. Yet few of us will have the time or the luxury to drink from it for long. It may be good that we can't.

Left to our own devices, we might choose to grieve for years. Why not? Our loss is deep, and we wonder how the world can go on when our hearts feel so empty. Like most luxuries, however, too much grief can make things worse. Given too much time and attention, our grief may become all-consuming and the master of our lives.

Today I want to grieve. Yet each day I sorrow, I am drawn farther and farther from reality. If this lasts too long, I will learn only to crave my world of sorrow more.

No. Like a warm coat in summer, grief has to be laid aside. Grief out of season becomes oppressive and burdensome. Sorrow, after a while, becomes an unwelcome guest.

The necessities of life call us to move on. There are bills to pay and carpets to vacuum. There are meals to prepare and shoes to shine. Boxes must be packed away. Final notes must be written or not written at all. It's time to put the lawnmower away and check the oil on the snowblower, whether we know how or not. Something needs to be done about the falling leaves.

Grief will have to move over now. Memories and reflections need to shift to the back row. Life rolls on, whether we want it to or not. The demands of the day call us to muster our courage.

Joab was told, "The king is weeping and mourning for [his son] Absalom." And ... the victory that day was turned into mourning, because on that day the troops heard it said, "The king is grieving for his son...."

Then Joab went into the house to the king and said, "Today you have humiliated all your men, who have just saved your life and the lives of your sons and daughters and the lives of your wives and concubines. ... Now go out and encourage your men. I swear by the Lord that if you don't go out, not a man will be left with you by nightfall. This will be worse for you than all the calamities that have come upon you from your youth till now."

So the king got up and took his seat in the gateway.

2 SAMUEL 19:1-8

Irish Wakes

❦

I tell you the truth,
if a man keeps my word,
he will never see death.

JOHN 8:51

I’ve never been to a wake, but I’ve heard stories. I’ve seen a couple in movies. Just enough to whet my curiosity. Somehow the idea of celebrating a person’s life at the time of his death has considerable appeal.

One has a feeling that a wake could put too much emphasis on alcohol, but I suppose not all are alike. There must be a dozen ways to rehearse good memories without having a headache afterward.

Too often funerals seem more intense and painful than they need to be. All of our concentration seems to be on the loss itself. Maybe more attention needs to be paid to the legacy of good times, helpfulness, and kindness that the person left along the path.

Most of us leave our mark on another life or two. A spouse. A child. A grandchild. A neighbor. Even strangers have benefited from our gentle voice or a word of advice from time to time. Most of us have touched someone as we have journeyed along.

This may be why stories mean so much. A handful of friends and relatives sitting around a room sharing happy memories can mean as much as any noisy party. There are stories that bring medicine to bleeding hearts. Stories about the child who once played in an open field. Stories of the young adult standing nervously at an altar. Stories about a parent crawling under a wooden porch to coax a cat out into the sunshine.

Too often we avoid mentioning the life of the person we cared about. It's as though we think we will be healthier if we hurry up and erase them from our minds.

Choking off memories can't begin to bless the image of someone who meant so very much. We all do better by cherishing the warm and cheerful moments that have been left behind.

When we laugh at memories of the dead, in a way we are laughing with them. Tears of sorrow and tears of joy look the same—they have no distinguishing marks, like different shapes or offsetting colors. Yet they are quite opposite. Tears of sorrow may be necessary. Tears of joy are more voluntary, the kind we need to give permission to before they flow easily.

Irish wakes seem to be an excellent way to let the joy pour out.

Old Wives' Tales

❧

O death, where then your victory?
Where then your sting?
1 CORINTHIANS 15:55, TLB

*D*on't talk about death or someone will die" is a saying my elderly aunt believes. Because she will not discuss death, she has a deep fear of it. It is sad to see her so anxious, as though to talk about death is a jinx.

For all her life she has chosen not to visit friends and relatives in nursing homes or during illnesses, because it makes her so uncomfortable. She rarely attends a funeral or goes to visitation at a funeral home.

Yet, my aunt misses so much by not being with her relatives when they are ill, and not sharing with the family at a death. How much happier she would be, how much calmer she could be, if she could become at ease with sickness and death. Since death is part of nature, to accept it helps to banish the fear.

Recently Bill and I planned to visit Costa Rica. At the time the only Spanish words I knew were "Buenos dias" and "Adios." As I thought of visiting a country where I could not understand or communicate with anyone, I became frightened and began to wonder if the trip was a good idea after all. Would I become lost and never get home again? Could we get to our hotels? Could we order food? Would someone rip us off as we handled foreign currency?

As my fears mounted, the solution became obvious: I needed to learn some Spanish. I called the local community college, found that a class was being taught that quarter, and enrolled right away. At the end of a nine-week session, I felt sufficiently prepared to make the trip. With my head filled with some basic Spanish vocabulary and my textbook in hand, I could hardly wait to explore Costa Rica.

There are numerous ways to become more comfortable with death and dying. There are many fine books. Churches and ministers can illuminate the subject. Being with friends as they face death and talking with loved ones can put us at ease. If we need special help, a good counselor can work with us.

Even though I walk
through the valley of the shadow of death,
I will fear no evil,
for you are with me;
your rod and your staff,
they comfort me.

PSALM 23:4

Win–Win

For to me, to live is Christ and to die is gain.
PHILIPPIANS 1:21

*O*ver the years I've tried to increase my faith by looking more closely at the life of Paul. No statement of his holds more power, hope, and purpose than this simple verse. It reflects an outlook on life that is a "win-win."

For Paul, it was good to stay in this world because he focused on his service to Christ as well as those to whom he ministered. This wasn't his favorite place to be, he made that clear, but he was committed to serving.

Given the choice, whether to stay or go, frankly Paul would rather have taken the next bus out (v. 23). However, he realized that it was necessary that he remain to help people like the believers at Philippi.

Thanks! I needed that. Paul's faith pulls me back

toward the middle, where I belong. There are many good reasons to be here. I can't afford to take my eyes off that. Yet Paul also helps me take a peek behind the curtain. Heaven is an even greater prize.

Life or death. It's a win-win situation.

Our faith in Christ certainly makes this picture complete. There is reason to believe that when we shake off this ailing, creaking body, we have a much better place to go. When we shed this bruised, unpredictable mind, there is a clearer way of thinking on the other side.

Our relatives can have the same expectation. That's why we so confidently say, while standing beside the casket, "She has finally laid down her burdens," or, "He has gone to a better place." We believe it is true.

Some days it might help to picture the person who has gone on to a "better place." We can imagine a smile on his face. Try to think of him not in a hospital bed or tied in a wheelchair but freely walking around, moving his arms, worshiping. This might be a good afternoon for him to go fishing.

Paul makes a big difference. He lifts our heads up high and turns our loss into a win-win.

No Easy Answers

Man of sorrows, acquainted with bitterest grief.
ISAIAH 53:3, TLB

*T*here are no easy funerals. Even if the person was old and ill, still the act of leaving this life and going to the next is sad. The separation, the memories, the emptiness—all are part of the process.

One funeral that was especially difficult was for a baby. The child had died in her sleep without any apparent cause. Bewildered and stricken, parents, grandparents, relatives, and friends were each left to go on without this young life, which had been snuffed out without cause or reason.

At the service the minister was straightforward and honest. His candor helped. He said there are two things we know about death, and little else.

First, we know that God is not responsible for the death. He isn't collecting cherubim or starting a children's choir. God loves his children, and he wanted these parents to raise this child.

Second, we know the parents are not responsible for the death. Their behavior in no way contributed to it. They had lovingly and carefully placed this infant in her crib, and the baby had died in her sleep. This was the same tender way they had laid the child down during the previous months.

Maybe someday, he went on, medicine would be able to explain how this child had died. But for now all we knew was what had not happened. We would only hurt ourselves by trying to attach blame where it did not belong. The minister continued to speak of hope and faith. He promised the parents that they would meet their child again someday at the feet of Christ.

Since the pastor knew he had few answers, he made it a point to dispel some errors instead. Removing the errors helped free the parents' souls.

It's a shame to watch someone bogged down after years of trying to find the answers. They cannot rise up and accept hope because they believe they must find all the pieces to the puzzle. The truth is this: The pieces to the puzzle may not exist. In all probability there is no way to complete this puzzle.

Since that is the case, it is time to appreciate the

picture for what it is: A beautiful landscape with five or ten pieces that will never be found. Accept the puzzle as complete, even though there are a few open spaces.

Hope and faith is what keeps us going even when we don't have all the answers. It is because of our faith that we are able to press on until we stand before the heavenly Father.

He Really Did Weep!

When Mary reached the place where Jesus was and saw him, she fell at his feet and said, "Lord, if you had been here, my brother would not have died."

When Jesus saw her weeping, and the Jews who had come along with her also weeping, he was deeply moved in spirit and troubled. "Where have you laid him?" he asked.

"Come and see, Lord," they replied.

Jesus wept.

JOHN 11:32-35

Which part of "Jesus wept" don't we understand? When Christ visited the tomb of his friend Lazarus, he saw Martha weeping. She grieved for her brother. In the midst of heartbroken relatives and friends, the Son of God shed tears as well.

Even though Jesus knew he would resurrect

142

Lazarus, and do it soon, he still cried. The perfect man, dealing with grief, did what came naturally to him.

Not everyone agrees with that interpretation. Some twist this passage like a pretzel and insist that Christ wept because of the ravages of sin and how sin separates us. OK. I can live with that. But I don't believe it.

Uncomfortable with the prospect of men crying, some might be a bit embarrassed that Christ would weep over death. Quite the contrary. I am very comfortable with the idea of God's Son having his heart broken along with the people he loves.

This biblical scene gives me permission (if I needed permission) to be natural. I don't have to stop and ask if it is proper to feel. It's completely normal to have a lump in my throat too big to swallow and too painful to ignore. The Jews standing by Jesus' side responded by saying, "See how he loved him."

Tears have a healthy role. They tend to clean out the eyes, reduce the swollen throat, and release tension. It is said that we either cry outside or cry inside. Those of us who cry outside are the lucky ones. We have done the healing thing.

To cry or not to cry is the question. Blessed are

those who don't need to answer it. They seem to allow their bodies to do whatever seems necessary.

We hear people say after loss:

"I wish I could have cried."

"I went off alone and cried."

"Months later I cried by myself."

"I don't know why, but I never did cry."

"I believe I did all my crying before she died."

Which is the right approach? Each and every one is good. Each person did what fit their mix, at the time or later. There are no formulas for crying. Each of us must respond in a way that is natural for us.

The Deepest Death

When people choose to take their own lives, they leave behind a trail of sorrow deeper than they ever imagined possible. Unfortunately, people who commit suicide have often told themselves exactly the opposite. Suicide victims first convince themselves that life will be better for everyone if they get out of the way.

There are exceptions. A few people kill themselves and make special effort to crush the ones they leave behind. Usually, however, this is not the case.

Often the victims not only feel worthless, but even believe their presence is harmful. They may picture their spouse marrying a terrific person and imagine their children playing cheerfully in the backyard of a large, expensive home. People who end their own lives usually are out of focus with reality.

Every mind is an island. None of us can fully understand how someone else thinks, rationalizes, and copes. Our ability to see inside another person's soul and spirit is limited to how much that person wants to let us in. The person who actually lives with that mind has enough trouble understanding. No one can know for sure what a person who committed suicide was thinking. That person is no longer here to explain.

Surviving family members and loved ones describe the experience as the deepest death. It is so painful because the suicide victim appears to have voluntarily decided to leave the people who cared for him or her. The message the survivors hear is "Your love wasn't strong enough to make me want to live." When they hear that message, people find it easy to believe they are worthless and somehow defective.

It is important to remember two facts that are true of most suicides.

First, the thinking of the one who died had become fuzzy. This person was having trouble working out the variables in his or her mind.

Second, the one who died had been having trouble communicating. If this person could have expressed him- or herself, the tragedy might have been avoided. Even words in suicide messages should be weighed with caution. Confused people tend to give confusing messages.

If someone leaves this life by suicide, the people

he or she has left behind need to find someone to whom they can talk. They only add to their pain by keeping their feelings inside. Those who are carrying this kind of grief need to find a friend, a relative, a minister, a counselor—anyone who will listen and offer the slightest encouragement. No closure is possible when a person kills him- or herself. The pain will always be there. However, the pain can become manageable if the survivors reach out for help.

It is sorrow and failure
which forces me to believe
that there is One who heareth prayer.

Charles Kingsley

Let's Make It Murder

*L*ast year I saw a movie I especially enjoyed. Already I've forgotten its name, and yet the storyline has been indelibly etched in my memory.

An elderly lady lived alone in a small southern town. Her bones ached, and her daily existence meant little to her. Bored and depressed, she took a pistol, lay across the bed, covered herself with a pillow, and shot herself.

When a niece found her dead she declared, "No member of our family has ever committed suicide." Immediately the relative set about rearranging the scene so that it would look like a murder. The story takes on excellent intrigue as people's lives are changed while the search goes on for the nonmurderer. Instead of accepting the facts head-on and dealing with the necessary healing, one gigantic game is invented involving the police and numerous innocent characters.

The inability or the unwillingness to handle reality can be the beginning of serious trouble. Every loss becomes incredibly more difficult if we pretend it is something else.

We call being fired "being laid off."

We refer to anger as "disappointment."

We call bankruptcy "re-careering."

We name tantrums merely "acting out."

When it comes to losses, a loss is a loss is a loss is a loss. No euphemism can decorate or camouflage the facts. Loss means something, or someone, is gone. Healthy grieving does not begin until we admit what has been lost.

If a child had a pet bird and that bird died, we would expect the child to somehow dispose of the feathered body. How terribly concerned we would be if the child either hid the dead creature or kept it in the cage and continued to talk to it. Children must learn to accept their losses.

We can understand why we are tempted to play games. None of us is eager to have what we care about taken away. How cold we would be if loss meant nothing to us.

Jesus talked about "whited sepulchres." They were graves painted over to look like they contained no death. One evidence of a sound mind is the acceptance of life and death as they actually are.

Too Busy to Grieve

❧

He that lacks time to mourn,
Lacks time to mend.

Sir Henry Taylor

When Emily's unmarried brother died, there was no one else to take direct responsibility for his arrangements, so his sister went right to work: there were people to call, decisions to make, and clothes to pick out. Anyone who has been there knows how exhausting this can be.

For two weeks she had remained near the dying forty-year-old night and day. Emily hardly noticed, but her body was more tired than she realized. Her own needs went unmet; so did the needs of her two children. Who had time to wash their clothes, comb their hair, and listen to them?

Burning energy day and night, eating if she could, she had no time to check her own gut reactions. Her brother had meant a great deal to her. There were mixed emotions, too, but she couldn't possibly find time to sift all of that out now.

Emily was on the run.

Weeks after the funeral, the devoted sister was carrying groceries into her kitchen when suddenly she collapsed into a chair. With cans of food rolling across the linoleum, Emily sobbed uncontrollably. The emotional dam broke, and all the grief she felt began to pour out.

Too often this happens to busy people. Well-meaning, kind individuals, they are able to run for only so long. Eventually the pain and the drain overcome them.

The old saying admonishes us to keep busy. That's true. But there's more to it. If the only thing we do is stay busy, grief is likely to overwhelm us.

Running to do things is sometimes just another way of running away. However, we can't run from grief forever. It has a knack for tracking us down and heading us off at the pass.

There is a sense in which most of us will collapse into the arms of God. Some do it sooner. Others do it later. Constant pain is bound to wear us out. Worn out, weak, and hurting, we need to find comfort in the Everlasting Arms.

It's OK to stay busy as much as it is all right to run away. But be careful. If we run too far and too hard, we might fall and get hurt.

Busy people are difficult to dissuade. Like marathon runners, they are compelled to push on. Fortunate are the few who will take time out to grieve at the beginning.

A Slice of the Pie

❧

When I have a friend over for coffee, I like to offer her a slice of pie. Not the entire pie. That's too much to eat at once, and the calories are astronomical. Just one slice, nice and warm from the oven, smelling of cinnamon goodness.

In a way, grief is a bit like that pie. When we are feeling loss and pain, we need to slice it up and dish some of it out to a friend or two. The majority will remain ours, but we would be making a mistake if we tried to eat it all by ourselves.

None of us should pass emotional pie around easily. Not everyone we know will want or accept it. Hand it out cautiously, but be certain to serve it to someone. If one friend will listen to us, we have dispensed, let us say, 10 percent. We still keep 90 percent, but that's a start. Dish up another 10 percent each to two more friends, and we still carry 70 percent with us. Seventy percent is definitely a bunch, but it is so much less than one hundred.

Don't worry about giving too many slices away.

As tightly as most of us are wrapped, there is little chance we will run out.

If we judiciously divide up a few pieces, we will reap some serious benefits. The greatest return may be that our friend will someday give us a slice of his or her pie. From time to time our friends will hurt in almost the same way that we hurt. They will need to share their pies, too.

So, share your pie. It could become one of those magic moments when a gift loosens up the receiver and takes him to new horizons.

What if a friend rejects the slice of our pie? How will we handle that awkward moment? Probably clumsily. That's the way most of us field grounders that take a bad hop. More often than not, however, our friends not only will accept the gift but will do so with a sense of honor. Our gesture says that we trust our friends with one of our most important possessions—sharing the pain and loss hiding close to our heart. Friends with sensitivity recognize this intimate contact for what it is.

Anyone who eats the entire pie alone could end up with any number of health problems. Serving others is more than a selfless act. This generosity opens avenues so that we will also receive emotional pie from others.

The next time you feel tears coming and struggle to hold them back, think of Mr. Bumbles' lines from Charles Dickens' Oliver Twist: "It opens the lungs, washes the countenance, exercises the eyes, and softens down the temper. So cry away!"

Dr. William H. Fey II

Not Invincible

On my bed I remember you;
I think of you through the watches of the night.
Because you are my help,
I sing in the shadow of your wings.
I stay close to you;
your right hand upholds me.

PSALM 63:6-8

*I*t comes at different ages for different people. For me it was at about age fifty-eight. Having enjoyed excellent health and never knowing aches and pains for all those years, I began to notice a change.

After long walks, soreness began to show up here and there, and my stamina was definitely decreasing. When driving at night I could tell that my vision was no longer perfect. I found I had to visit the doctor and dentist more frequently.

That's when, for the first time, I thought, "It's true. I'm not invincible. Someday I'll be incapacitated like my neighbor. I will probably be hospitalized and have to undergo all sorts of procedures like my cousin. I will have to give up my independence as my elderly friends have done. And finally, I will die. Change and dying are part of nature."

Life can be compared to the four quarters of a football game. I am definitely in the fourth quarter.

Recently Bill and I spent an evening talking about what is ahead for us. We talked about life, death, separation, and heaven. We don't know how the fourth quarter will play out, but it helped to share what we have learned and believe about aging, death, and heaven.

It was reassuring to discuss what Jesus said about heaven, and it is comforting to know that our heavenly Father is in charge and will heartily welcome us to his home.

All of us are dying; it is the final stage of life. Since our bodies are made to end, when health is gone I believe we will wish for and welcome death.

I ran from grief;
grief ran and overtook me.

Francis Quarles

People With Gray Hair

❧

I know it's not easy to focus on something else when your body aches. But it's important to try. Preoccupation with your ailment makes you a prisoner of your body because the body is then dictating your whole life; in turn, your whole life starts to revolve around injury or dysfunction or deficiency. There are healthier and more pleasing ways to spend your efforts and energy.

Morrie Schwartz

Seeing the silver in my hair reminds me how much I have been blessed. That's the only way we get this far. Millions don't make it. No matter how much calamity or distress has filled our lives, the advent of graying hair is testimony to the fact that God has been good.

Despite all of my denials, I am not like I was at

age eighteen. The wrinkles are there, along with the slightly ashen tint. I can't run or hit fly balls like I used to.

My energy level isn't quite the same. Recently I tried to stuff my medicine into a plastic container to take with me on a trip. There were so many pills I had to get a second container. Now I carry all of them in a zippered bag.

Aging has many benefits, too many to list on this page. One of its best rewards is the clear message that my life has passed the halfway point. I don't feel like death is near, but I can see it in the distance.

Most of us have taken those long trips where, after traveling up and down so many hilly roads, suddenly, far away, we see the mountains. The mountains are beautiful, awesome, and majestic. It will take some time to get there, but we become almost breathless at the sight.

I don't know how many miles I have yet to travel, but I can see the mountains from here. It's time to start soaking in some of the wonders. Death is becoming a reality. I can start drinking in some of its splendor.

If I had died as a teen, mangled in a twisted wreck along the highway, I never could have contemplated my own demise. A heart attack at age fifty while walking along the sidewalk may have its benefits, but it robs one of so much. Fortunately and gratefully I have lived long enough to see the definite signs, and I have an idea of what is going to happen.

I know I will not live to be 120. I also know that at the present rate of gradual decay I don't want to live that long. Frankly I wouldn't mind 98 or so, but only if I could still learn from children.

Dutifully I will continue to take the pills and head out for regular walks, but every once in a while my body sends me another quiet message. God is gently but steadily reminding me that the mountains get a little closer every day.

Death is only an old door
set in a garden wall.

Edna St. Vincent Millay

I think of death as a glad awakening
from this troubled sleep which we call life;
as an emancipation from the world
which, beautiful though it be,
is still a land of captivity.

Lyman Abbott

In extreme youth, in our most humiliating
sorrow, we think we are alone.
When we are older we find that others have
suffered too.

Suzanne Moarny

The Chair in the Hall

Not only is the old chair the first thing you notice when you come into the house, it also cost a pretty penny. A decorative item, rarely does anyone actually sit in it. It belongs in the hallway, everyone knows it's there, and yet seldom is it used.

Occasionally, when the entire family comes over or when the women's group shows up, the chair is retrieved from the hall. Uncle Ben or Mrs. Showalter then spends a long evening in it. Afterward the high-back floral piece is returned to its allotted space.

Sometimes our faith is very much like that chair. It's definitely there. It's not quite taken for granted, yet neither is it in the main room. Faith has a designated spot, and everyone knows where it belongs.

Then, unexpectedly (or expectedly), some kind of hardship comes to visit. A painful loss arrives uninvited, leaving us weak, exhausted, and stunned. Automatically we reach for the chair in the hall, pull it close, and sit down.

Our faith is a familiar chair, but in loss we sit on it

as we have never sat before. We sit a bit lower, a bit heavier, a little less erect. Our soul doesn't sit up quite as straight. Our spirit needs the entire chair for support.

What will happen now that we need the chair so much? Will it hold us? Is it large enough to take all our weight? Is it wide enough for every experience? Are the arms sturdy? Can we let go of ourselves and feel confident the chair of faith will do its job?

Don't be surprised if it seems uncomfortable at first. Never before have we needed to use so much of the chair to hold us so completely.

Are the legs more wobbly than we remember? That's all right. They still hold, even if they creak a tad. The chair we sat in the day the newborn baby came home from the hospital is the same chair we sat in when Dad lost his job. The chair has the same strength on the good days that it has on the bad.

We shouldn't be surprised if we hear it squeak. If the old back gives a fraction of an inch, don't give up on it too quickly. Settle in. Stay until you begin to feel its full comfort again. Soon you will realize that this chair will not let you down.

But we do see Jesus—who for awhile was a little lower than the angels—crowned now by God with glory and honor because he suffered death for us.

HEBREWS 2:9, TLB

The Bible tells us, and tells us clearly, that by the death of Jesus Christ on a cross, death itself has been conquered, its bitter sting has been removed, and in a day yet to be, it will be destroyed.

Joseph Bayly

No, in all these things we are more than conquerors
through him who loved us.
For I am convinced that
neither death nor life,
neither angels nor demons,
neither the present nor the future,
nor any powers,
neither height nor depth,
nor anything else in all creation,
will be able to separate us
 from the love of God that is in Christ Jesus our
   Lord.

ROMANS 8:37-39